THE ARTFUL ASTROLOGER

SAGITTARIUS

Lee Holloway

Gramercy Books
New York • Avenel

To my children

A Friedman Group Book

Copyright ©1993 by Michael Friedman Publishing Group
All rights reserved.

This 1993 edition is published by Gramercy Books,
distributed by Outlet Book Company, Inc.,
a Random House Company, 40 Engelhard Avenue,
Avenel, New Jersey 07001.

Printed and bound in Singapore

Library of Congress Cataloging–in–Publication Data

Holloway, Lee.
      The artful astrologer. Sagittarius / by Lee Holloway.
         p. cm.
     ISBN 0-517-08258-6
     1. Sagittarius (Astrology)   I. Title.
    BF1727.6H65   1993
    133.5'2—dc20   93-24878
                                   CIP

8 7 6 5 4 3 2 1

CONTENTS

Symbolic rendering of a seventeenth-century astrologer.

INTRODUCTION

Is astrology bunk, or is there something to it? If astrology is utter nonsense, why have so many of the world's finest thinkers, including Johannes Kepler, Copernicus, Isaac Newton, Carl Jung, and Goethe, turned to astrology for information and guidance over the centuries?

Some people may scoff when astrology is mentioned, but even these skeptics are usually inquisitive about their signs. Whenever I attend a dinner party, I ask the host not to mention that I am an astrologer—at least not until dessert—because the conversation invariably turns to astrolo-

In the middle ages, the wealthy consulted astrologers regularly.

gy. When people learn that I am an astrologer, they first try to get me to tell them about their signs and what lies in store for them. Then, in a subtle way, they bring up the next bit of business, which usually concerns a loved one. Finally, as you've probably guessed, they want to know whether the two signs get along.

We humans are an inquisitive lot—we are eager to learn more about our friends, family, lovers, and employers. Astrology is one way to satisfy that natural curiosity.

In the not too distant past, only royalty, heads of state, and the very rich consulted with astrologers; such consultation was a privilege of the elite. Today, astrology is a source of information and fascination for millions; astrological columns can be found in major newspapers and magazines all over the world.

Astrology is not a form of magic. It is a science. Put simply, it is a practical application of astronomy that links the stars and planets with our daily lives. A horoscope is a picture of the stars and planets at a given time, such as that of a person's birth. By examining each planet's position and the relationships of all of the planets to each other at a specific moment, an astrologer can determine your basic personality or predict a general course of events. Perhaps the noted Swiss psychologist Carl Jung summed up the concept of astrology best when he said, "Whatever is born or done at this moment, has the qualities of this moment in time." Astrologers form a continuous link with the past, and each human being, although unique, is part of nature and the universe.

Unfortunately, some people have the misconception that astrology dictates who they are and how their life has to be.

This chart dates back to fourteenth-century Italy. The inside circles represent the element, ruling body part, and orientation of each respective sign.

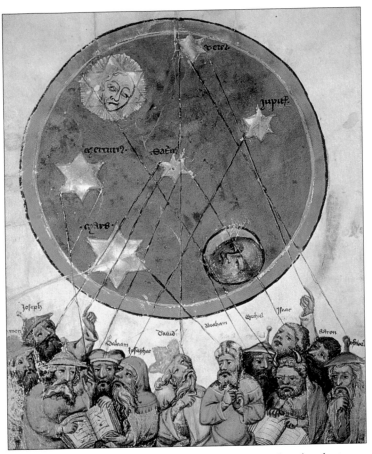

Medieval illuminated manuscript of biblical characters observing the stars.

Nothing could be further from the truth. Astrology does not remove our free will; it simply points out our basic nature and how we are likely to react in certain circumstances. Astrology indicates strengths and weaknesses, talents and abilities, difficulties and opportunities. It is always up to the individual to use this information, and to live his or her life accordingly, or to disregard it.

Like other sciences, astrology's origins date back thousands of years. There is evidence that primitive peoples recorded the phases of the Moon by carving notches on reindeer bones, and that they may have linked the Moon's movement with the tides, or the snow's melting in spring with the rising of the constellation now known as Aries. As early as 2000 B.C., astrologers were using instruments—carved out of granite or fashioned from brass or copper—to observe and calculate the positions of constellations. These calculations were surprisingly accurate, even by today's standards.

Over time, astrological calculations were refined and the planets were named. The Babylonians were the first to describe the natural zodiac, and their first horoscope dates back to 409 B.C. Centuries ago, people began to examine the stars' potential impact on human emotions, spirit, and intellect. Today, astrology is so deeply embedded in our culture and language that we rarely give it a second thought. The

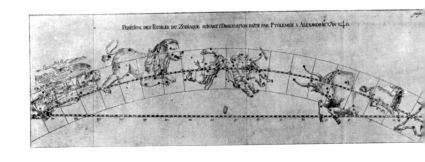

POSITION DES ETOILES DU ZODIAQUE suivant l'Observation faite par Ptolemée à Alexandrie l'An 140.

The twelve zodiacal constellations as drawn according to Ptolemy's descriptions.

days of the week , for example, have their roots in astrology. Sunday is derived from "Sun Day," Monday from "Moon Day," Tuesday from "Tiwe's Day," Wednesday from "Woden's Day," Thursday from "Thor's Day," Friday from "Frigga's Day," and Saturday from "Saturn's Day." Lunacy, which originally referred to so-called full-moon madness, now encompasses all varieties and forms of mental illness.

Before we begin, I'd like to touch upon one final point. Throughout this book, you'll see references to "rulers." A ruler, in astrological terms, has the same meaning as it does in human society; "ruler" refers to the planet that governs or co-governs an astrological sign (see pages 14–15) or to the constellation rising at the birth of a person or event. Everything has a moment of birth: people, places, profes-

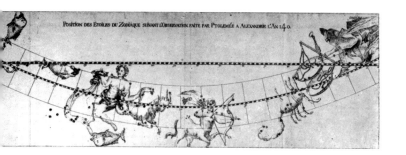

Position des Étoiles du Zodiaque suivant l'observation faite par Ptolemée à Alexandrie l'An 140.

sions, even ideas; it would take volumes to show you what persons, places, and things your sign rules, but a small sampling has been included here. For example, different parts of the body have rulers, and that body part is often a point of strength and weakness. Gemstones and colors have also been assigned to each sign, although there are varying opinions about the validity of these less important areas. (It should also be noted here that the gemstone assigned to a particular sign does not correspond to the birthstone assigned to that month.) Generally, however, colors and gemstones are said to reflect the specific energy of each sign.

May *The Artful Astrologer* enlighten and entertain you.

Lee Holloway

THE PLANETS

The **SUN** symbolizes the life force that flows through everything. It rules the sign of Leo and represents ego, will, identity, and consciousness.

The **MOON** symbolizes emotions and personality. It rules the sign of Cancer and represents feeling, instinct, habit, childhood, mother, sensitivity, and receptivity.

MERCURY symbolizes the mind and communication. It rules the signs of Gemini and Virgo and represents thought, learning, communication, reason, speech, youth, and perception.

VENUS symbolizes love and attraction. It rules the signs of Taurus and Libra and represents harmony, values, pleasure, comfort, beauty, art, refinement, and balance.

MARS symbolizes action and drive. It rules the sign of Aries and represents energy, the sex drive, initiative, the ability to defend oneself, resilience, and conflict.

JUPITER symbolizes expansion and growth. It rules the sign of Sagittarius and represents higher thought and learning, principles, beliefs, optimism, abundance, idealism, and morals.

SATURN symbolizes universal law and reality. It rules the sign of Capricorn and represents structure, discipline, limitation, restriction, fear, authority figures, father, teachers, and time.

*The nine planets that comprise our solar system: Mercury, Venus, Earth,
Mars, Saturn, Jupiter, Uranus, Neptune, and Pluto.*

URANUS symbolizes individuality and change. It rules the sign
of Aquarius and represents intuition, genius, insight, reform,
unconventionality, and freedom.

NEPTUNE symbolizes compassion and spirituality. It rules the
sign of Pisces and represents the search for the divine, intuition,
dreams, illusion, imagination, and confusion.

PLUTO symbolizes transformation and regeneration. It rules the
sign of Scorpio and represents power, death and rebirth, the
subconscious, elimination, obsession, and purging.

THE ZODIAC SIGNS

Just as there are twelve months in the year, there are twelve astrological signs in the zodiac. The word "zodiac" comes from the Greek *zoidiakos*, which means "circle of animals" and refers to a band of fixed stars that encircles the earth. The twelve signs are divided into four elements: fire, air, earth, and water. The three signs within an element share many similarities, but each sign in the zodiac is unique. The following section is a brief summary of the qualities of the signs born under each element. (The terms "positive" and "negative" as they are used here describe qualities, and are not judgments.)

The fire signs are Aries, Leo, and Sagittarius. They are termed positive and extroverted. They are warm, creative, outgoing, expressive, idealistic, inspirational, and enthusiastic.

The air signs are Gemini, Libra, and Aquarius. They are termed positive and extroverted. They are social, outgoing, objective, expressive, and intellectual.

The earth signs are Taurus, Virgo, and Capricorn. They are termed negative and introverted. They are practical, conservative, reserved, traditional, and deliberate.

The water signs are Cancer, Scorpio, and Pisces. They are termed negative and introverted. They are sensitive, emotional, imaginative, and intuitive.

The fire signs:

Aries   Leo   Sagittarius

The air signs:

Gemini   Libra   Aquarius

The earth signs:

Taurus   Virgo   Capricorn

The water signs:

Cancer   Scorpio   Pisces

Sagitt

Symbol: Centaur

Planetary ruler: Jupiter

Element: Fire

Rules in the body: Thighs

Day of the week: Thursday

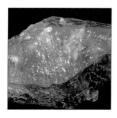

Gem: Sapphire

Color: Deep blue

Key words: I aspire

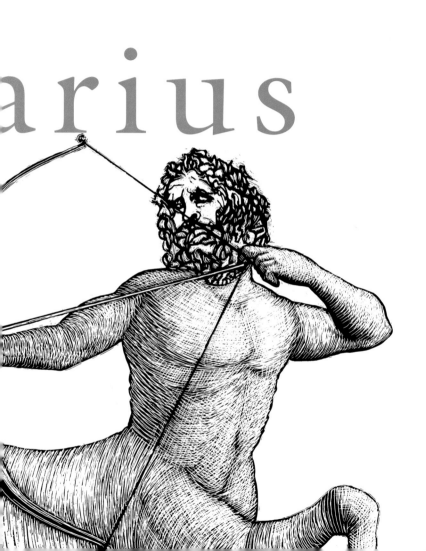

YOUR SUN SIGN PROFILE

Are you the kind of person who at a party seems to have one foot out the door but yet doesn't leave? Since freedom is the Sagittarian's credo and is as natural to this sign as breathing, you will always seem to be checking the exits in life; in your own way, you are somewhat claustrophobic.

Like a wild horse, a Sagittarian needs to be free to thrive, and that freedom must be both mental and physical. You simply have to know that freedom is somewhere out there, and that it's yours whenever you want it. It's not so much that you will always run away if given the chance; in fact, you probably won't go anywhere. You just need to feel that you are free to do as you please, when you please. This is one of the most important things about a Sagittarian. If someone tries to tie you down or fence you in, the last thing he or she will see is a cloud of dust; although it may take some time for you to leave, in the end you will—one way or another.

Sagittarius is ruled by Jupiter, the luckiest and largest planet in our solar system, which may account for your somewhat reckless and expansive nature. Who else but a Sagittarian would throw caution to the wind, confident that jolly old Jove will make everything come out right in the end? And more often than not, things just seem to work out. "Eleventh-Hour Luck" should be Sagittarius' nickname, for as sure as spring follows

Due to its high internal temperature, Jupiter, Sagittarius' planetary ruler, gives off about 65 percent more heat than it absorbs from the Sun, because Jupiter is cooling and its gaseous atmosphere is condensing—a process that began when the planet was formed.

winter, someone up there is definitely looking out for him or her. Some Sagittarian luck is self-made through a friendly, optimistic outlook, but Jupiter's benevolent and lucky influence helps a lot, too.

A Sagittarius is a mixture of teacher, preacher, prophet, and court jester, and some of these qualities shine forth regardless of your chosen profession. No one loves to teach, preach, or inspire others more, for Sagittarius rules

WHAT SONG WAS SUNG BY A FAMOUS SAGITTARIAN, WITH LYRICS THAT BEST CAPTURE THE SIGN'S ESSENCE?

"The Impossible Dream," Sammy Davis, Jr.

wisdom, prophecy, principles, religion, and ethics. Sagittarians can pontificate at the drop of a hat and do so frequently, often giving advice without being asked. Others seem not to mind because of Sagittarians' great sense of humor and enthusiasm. People are energized by their cheerful and positive views. Sagittarians also have a natural gift of intuition that usually increases with use.

Sagittarians can and frequently do have stunning intelligences, due to their philosophical planetary ruler; this is why so many of them excel in intellectual careers. It's no wonder that Sagittarians' key words are "I aspire." If they learn to master their "foot-in-mouth" tendencies, they can aspire to and attain great professional heights. The careers they are most suited to are teacher, professor, lawyer, preacher, lecturer, writer, publisher, bookseller, and travel agent.

Sagittarians are perennial students, which may account for the youthfulness they retain throughout their lives. They also thrive on challenges that force them to utilize their intellect to its fullest. Although you can probably master various games, it

Sagittarians are noted for their great energy and charisma, two traits Tina Turner has brought to the stage as one of soul's hottest performers.

Disney

is likely that it is the game of life that excites you most.

In matters of love and romance, Sagittarians simply can't stand jealousy or possessiveness. They can be inventive and passionate lovers, as long as they can maintain their sense of freedom and independence. Sagittarians desire partners with whom they can travel down the road of life without feeling shackled. Humor and playfulness are natural expressions of their romantic nature. They frequently fall in love with and marry a friend, but many choose to remain single because of that ever-powerful need for freedom. If a Sagittarian marches down the aisle, it is certain that he or she

Beethoven

Sinatra

either has been drugged or, more likely, is completely enchanted.

The surprising thing about Sagittarians, however, is that they can and do make wonderful marriage partners, even with that compulsive streak of independence. If their partners stand back, give them breathing room, and let them know they want to share in their adventures, not confine

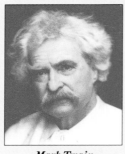

Mark Twain

or limit them, they can offer some of the most fun-filled relationships imaginable. Life with a Sagittarius will probably be mixed with long philosophical talks, travel, and lots of laughter, often at himself or herself, and life.

Like every sign, Sagittarius has positive and negative attributes, and the ability to choose which qualities to express. As a Sagittarian, you should be aware that if your enthusiasm carries you away, others may see you as flighty or unreliable. You may promise things you can't deliver and be off to explore the next horizon before taking care of matters at hand. If you are a typical Sagittarian, you may have to develop more discipline and learn to evaluate your ability to fulfill obligations before committing to them. With so much energy and natural good fortune at your disposal, the few lessons you may have to learn in contemplation and completion will go a long way toward helping you achieve your goals.

COMPATIBILITY

In nature, some elements are more compatible and blend more easily than others, like fire and air, and earth and water; the same holds true in astrology. Therefore, some astrological signs naturally interact more harmoniously than others.

The information in this section describes how Sagittarius tends to relate to other signs. It provides guidelines to the potential strengths and weaknesses of a relationship between two signs. But remember, these are only guidelines. In the final analysis, the choice is yours.

As a fire sign, Sagittarius is most compatible with the other fire signs, Leo and Aries. The natural rapport of the fire signs stems from their many emotional and intellectual similarities.

The air signs Aquarius and Libra are also suitable partners for Sagittarius. Although Gemini is also an air sign, it is Sagittarius' opposite in the zodiac, so the relationship would be a bit more challenging than one with either of the other air signs. In nature "air fans fire, and fire warms air," and the same is true in astrology. This is the reason fire and air signs are basically compatible.

The earth signs—Taurus, Capricorn, and Virgo—are not as compatible with Sagittarius as the fire and air signs, for earth signs tend to lack the spontaneity and penchant for exploration that attracts Sagittarius. The earth signs thrive on order and would find Sagittarius' need for freedom and more reckless nature unsettling.

Because of their basic elemental differences, the water signs—Cancer, Scorpio, and Pisces—are less suitable partners for Sagittarius. Water can dampen fire's enthusiasm, while fire can prove to be too much for water's sensitivity. Fire and water can be a steamy, combustible combination, but one that is more turbulent than peaceful.

Single, in control of her film career, and owner of a small town in Georgia, Kim Basinger exudes Sagittarian independence.l

As the travelers of the zodiac, Sagittarians love to explore new roads, and Jimi Hendrix, in terms of his music, riveting performances, and flamboyant manner of dress, was no exception.

LEO AND SAGITTARIUS

 Because they are both warm and affectionate, Leo (July 24–August 23) and Sagittarius make wonderful partners. Leos take themselves much too seriously at times, so Sagittarian humor is just the ticket to help them laugh their way back to reality. Leo, of course, can help to stabilize Sagittarius' energy, which can be a little scattered. A Sagittarian often looks to the future before taking care of the present, so steady, determined Leo can act as ballast in Sagittarius' restless life. As long as Sagittarius pays enough attention to Leo and is very, very careful not to wound the Lion's tremendous pride, these two can forge one of the happiest unions in the zodiac.

ARIES AND SAGITTARIUS

 Aries (March 21–April 20) and Sagittarius are also highly compatible, since they both love change and adventure. It will sometimes be hard to tell which of the two is more childlike, but on the whole this can be a dynamite connection. Sagittarius is the Pied Piper of the zodiac, offering dreams and philosophy that can bewitch Aries, while Aries has the drive and initiative to make dreams come true. The dynamic pairing of Jupiter and Mars, Sagittarius' and Aries' ruling planets, makes this an unstoppable twosome when they combine their energies toward achieving a single goal. There will

WOODY ALLEN'S HUMOR IS TRULY SAGITTARIAN. AS THE PHILOSOPHER-JOKER ONCE SAID:

More than any other time in history, mankind faces a crossroads. One path leads to despair and utter hopelessness. The other, to total extinction. Let us pray we have the wisdom to choose correctly.

—*Side Effects* (1980), "My Speech to Graduates"

Woody Allen

always be a level of excitement between these two highly charged fire signs, whether their relationship is a romantic or business-related one.

SAGITTARIUS AND SAGITTARIUS

Two Sagittarians are a good match because of their similar natures. The problems these two face arise mainly from their need for independence and their desire to be always on the go. (One wonders if they will ever be home long enough to work on a relationship!) When they finally do end up across from each other at the dinner table, they will enjoy sharing entertaining stories about their latest adventures and will try desperately to find some philosophical meaning to it all.

AQUARIUS AND SAGITTARIUS

 Aquarius (January 20–February 18) and Sagittarius are a nice pairing. Sagittarians have more difficulty settling down than almost any other sign—except Aquarians. Even when a Sagittarian commits to someone, he or she prefers to retain some level of independence. Fortunately, Aquarius also prefers not to be tied down, at least not in a conventional way. And Aquarius doesn't go along with the establishment, which doesn't upset freedom-loving Sagittarius. Aquarius and Sagittarius can obviously form a happy, productive union.

LIBRA AND SAGITTARIUS

 A relationship between Libra (September 23–October 22) and Sagittarius brings together two of the most beneficial ruling planets in the zodiac, Jupiter and Venus. This can be a winning combination, both romantically and professionally. Sagittarius is by nature expansive and optimistic, and Libra has charm, style, and intellect. Libra can be too indecisive at times, while Sagittarius loves to give advice and direction. Libra also likes to please others,

The relationship between baseball legend Joe DiMaggio (Sagittarius) and eternal sex goddess Marilyn Monroe (Gemini) is a good example of the potential interaction between those born under these two signs. Because they were polar opposites, the sexual attraction between the two was immediate and strong (Marilyn later remarked to Truman Capote about the relationship that if satisfying sex was "all it takes, we'd still be married."). The marriage failed primarily because Monroe thrived on attention, socializing, and her evolving career (all part of the Gemini focus), while DiMaggio was more introverted and shunned the limelight. Nonetheless, DiMaggio remained a devoted friend (typical of Sagittarius) to Monroe: he helped her through various personal difficulties and sent roses to her grave every week for more than two decades after her death.

sometimes at the cost of his or her own feelings and desires. Sagittarius' highly adaptable nature should make it easier for Libra to say what he or she feels and to act according to his or her true wishes.

GEMINI AND SAGITTARIUS

Gemini (May 22–June 21) is the polar opposite of Sagittarius, and in astrology opposites often attract. Both Gemini and Sagittarius love to learn. Gemini has a great curiosity and loves trivia and diverse facts, while Sagittarius is interested only in understanding the whole picture and how all the elements work together. Gemini is a cool, mental sign, and Sagittarius is an expressive, emotional sign. This twosome can balance each other's energy, but only if they accept and adjust to their differences.

TAURUS AND SAGITTARIUS

Taurus (April 21–May 21) is as solid as a rock and about as flexible. Sagittarius is highly changeable, takes risks, and acts impulsively. Taurus needs time to plan and to assimilate experiences, while Sagittarius has only two gears—fast and forward. Many adjustments will be required for this union to work.

CAPRICORN AND SAGITTARIUS

 Capricorn (December 22–January 19) is another less than favorable match for Sagittarius. Here, there can be some meeting of the minds, particularly in business, rather than in romance, but on the whole these two are very different souls. Capricorn is reserved, sometimes shy, and always saving for a rainy day. Sagittarius is extroverted, loves people, and doesn't believe in rainy days. These two can make for an interesting duo if Sagittarius draws upon his or her sense of humor, and Capricorn upon his or her wisdom—gifts from the gods to each.

SOME CITIES RULED BY SAGITTARIUS

Avignon, France
Branford, England
Cologne, Germany
Narbonne, France
Nottingham, England
Toledo, Ohio
Toronto, Canada

The Toronto skyline.

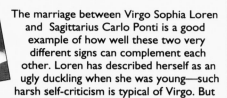

The marriage between Virgo Sophia Loren and Sagittarius Carlo Ponti is a good example of how well these two very different signs can complement each other. Loren has described herself as an ugly duckling when she was young—such harsh self-criticism is typical of Virgo. But Ponti apparently saw her potential, which perhaps could be attributed to his optimistic, confident Sagittarian nature. They worked together on a number of films, the first of which was *Girls Marked For Danger* (1952), and Ponti helped her to develop the self-assurance she needed to succeed as an actress. She, in turn, helped ground the independent Ponti, providing a solid home base for him. The rest, as they say, is history.

VIRGO AND SAGITTARIUS

Virgo (August 24–September 22) and Sagittarius are unlikely bedfellows. Virgo is introverted and concentrates on the details of life; Sagittarius is extroverted and cares mainly about the grand scheme of things. This is not an impossible pairing, but it's not an easy one, either. Virgos tend to worry too much, and Sagittarians too little. However, Virgo's penchant for the nitty-gritty works well with Sagittarius' tendency to "not sweat the small stuff." Virgo's role in life is generally that of the caretaker, so if Virgos throw their lot in with this restless sign, they will have their work cut out for them.

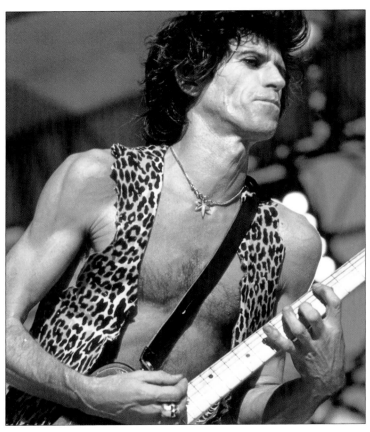

Keith Richards is a true outspoken Sagittarius; he has talked openly to the press about topics that range form the sudden death of his infant son to his relationship with fellow Stone Mick Jagger.

Cancer and Sagittarius

 The life of lunar-ruled Cancer (June 22–July 23) is run by feelings. No other sign of the zodiac expresses such a roller coaster of emotions—Cancers are up one moment, down the next. The word that best describes Cancer is sensitive. Cancer is also the sign that rules home and hearth, while Sagittarius could be called the sign that rules wanderlust. Sagittarius is notorious for slip-of-the-lip comments that unintentionally offend, and Cancer takes things so personally that many hurt feelings could arise in this association. However, there is much potential for happiness here. Sagittarians can use humor to help Cancers laugh through their tears, while Cancers can nurture Sagittarians when they're blue and provide a solid home base for them. But on the whole, if this relationship is to work, each partner will have to curb innate qualities that can offend the other.

COUNTRIES RULED BY SAGITTARIUS

Australia
Chile
Hungary
Madagascar

Australia's famous Ayers Rock.

Bette Midler